2000-20
BEST MOVIE M
TEN YEARS OF SHEET MUSIC HITS!

OCAL

Produced by
Alfred Music Publishing Co., Inc.
P.O. Box 10003
Van Nuys, CA 91410-0003
alfred.com

Printed in USA.

ISBN-10: 0-7390-6883-0
ISBN-13: 978-0-7390-6883-0

 Alfred Cares. Contents printed on 100% recycled paper.

CONTENTS

9000 DAYS

(from *Invictus*)

Lyrics by
DINA EASTWOOD and
EMILE WELMAN

Music by
CLINT EASTWOOD and
MICHAEL STEVENS

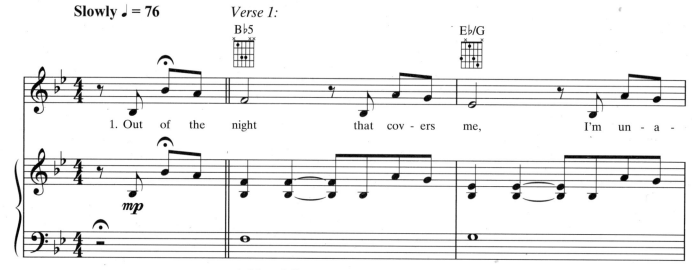

ACROSS THE STARS

(Love Theme from *Star Wars®: Episode II, Attack Of The Clones*)

Music by
JOHN WILLIAMS

Moderately slow & gently (♩ = 76)

(with pedal)

Appassionato

ADELIELAND

(from *Happy Feet*)

By JOHN POWELL

Moderately bright latin ♩ = 132

Adelieland - 3 - 1

AHSOKA'S TRIUMPHANT THEME

(from *Star Wars: The Clone Wars*)

By KEVIN KINER

AL OTRO LADO DEL RÍO

(from *The Motorcycle Diaries*)

Letra y Música por
JORGE ABNER DREXLER

ALL IS LOVE

(from *Where the Wild Things Are*)

Words and Music by
KAREN O and NICK ZINNER

26

All Is Love - 5 - 4

AMERICA'S AVIATION HERO

(from *The Aviator*)

By
HOWARD SHORE

Moderately (♩ = 88)

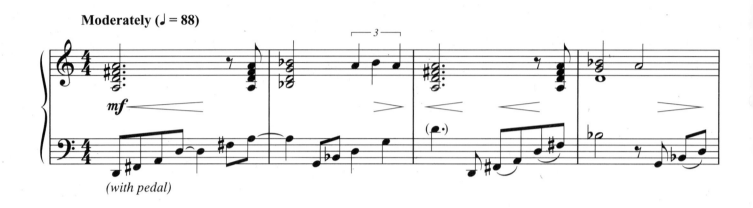

(with pedal)

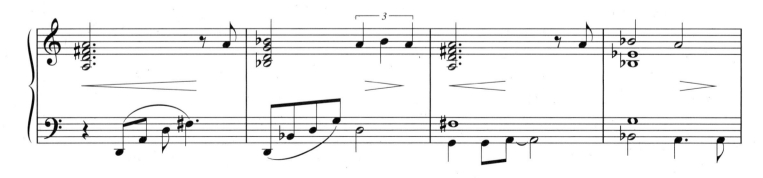

America's Aviation Hero - 2 - 1

Appassionata

AT LAST
(from *Cadillac Records*)

Lyric by
MACK GORDON

Music by
HARRY WARREN

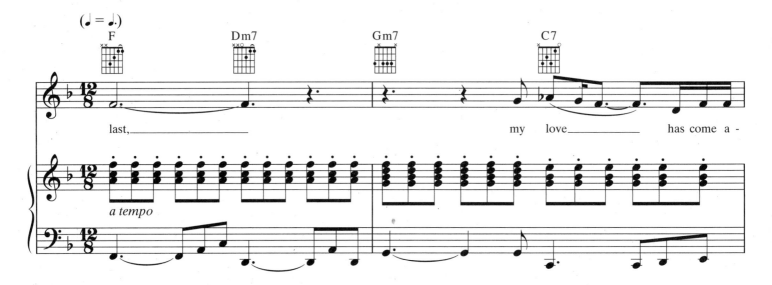

At Last - 5 - 1

Lyrics: long. My lone-ly days are o-ver and life is like a song. Oh, yeah, yeah. At last, the skies above are

At Last - 5 - 2

AUGUST RUSH RHAPSODY
(Piano Suite)

Composed by
MARK MANCINA
Arranged by DAVE METZGER

Gently (♩. = 54)
"Main Theme"

August Rush Rhapsody (Piano Suite) - 5 - 1

Delicately ($\quarternote$ = 80)

"August's Theme"

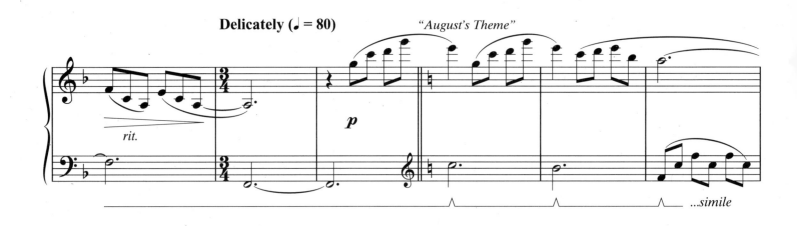

(a bit more deliberately)

"Parents Theme"

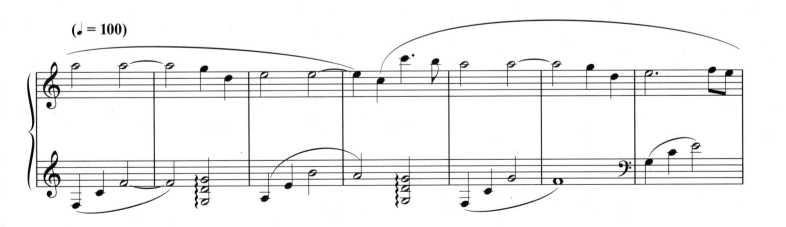

BELIEVE
(from *The Polar Express*)

Words and Music by
ALAN SILVESTRI and GLEN BALLARD

Moderately slow ♩ = 80

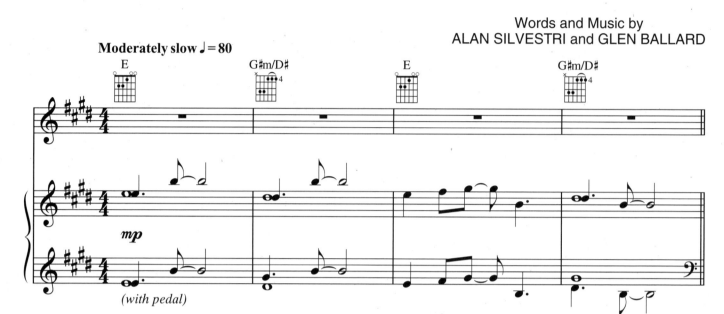

(with pedal)

Verse:

1. Chil - dren___ sleep - ing,___ snow is soft - ly fall - ing.___
2. Trains move___ quick - ly___ to their jour - ney's end.

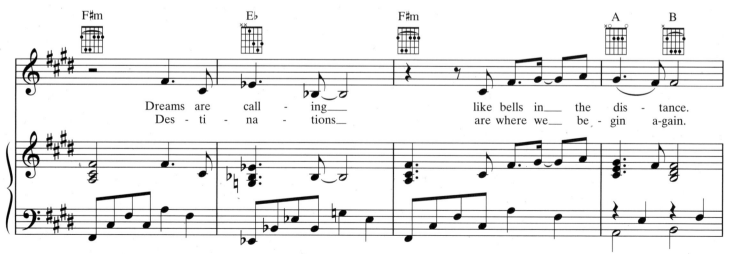

Dreams are call - ing___ like bells in___ the dis - tance.
Des - ti - na - tions___ are where we___ be - gin a-gain.

Believe - 4 - 1

BILLY'S THEME

(from *The Departed*)

By HOWARD SHORE

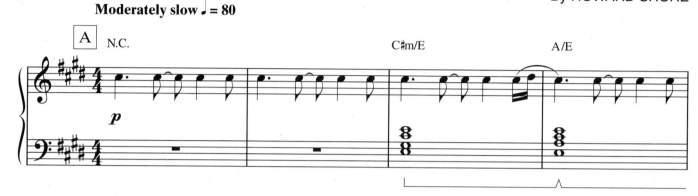

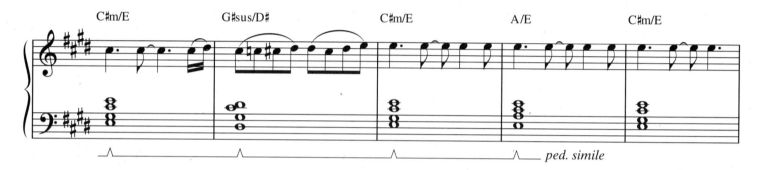

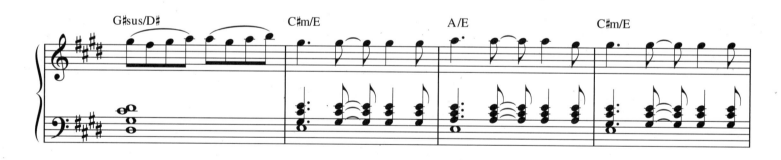

Billy's Theme - 7 - 1

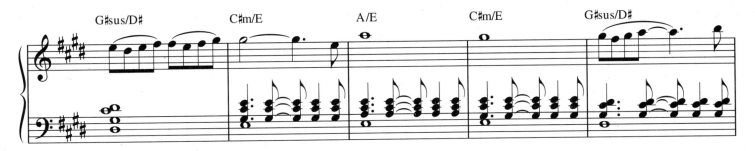

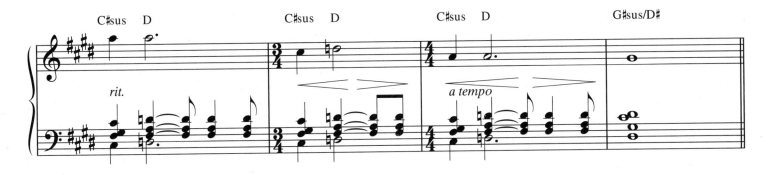

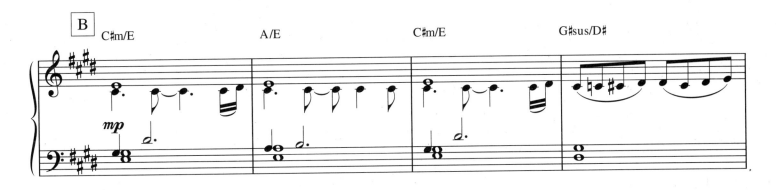

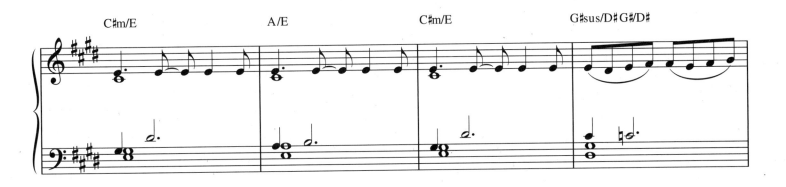

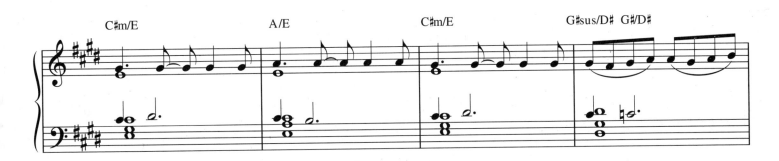

46

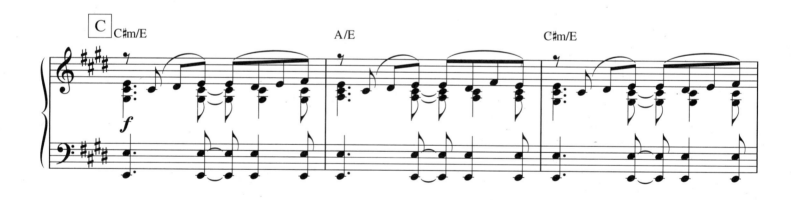

Billy's Theme - 7 - 3

48

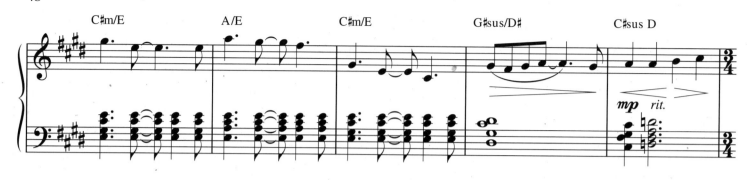

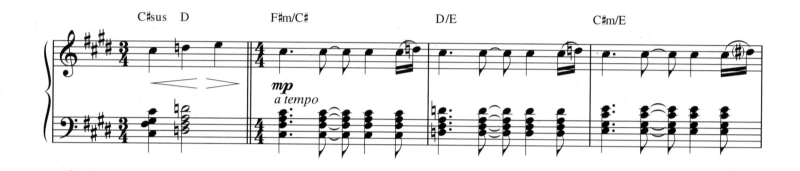

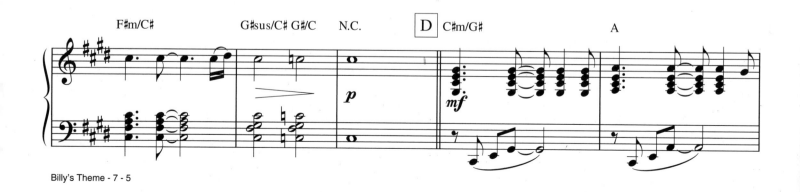

Billy's Theme - 7 - 5

Billy's Theme - 7 - 6

50

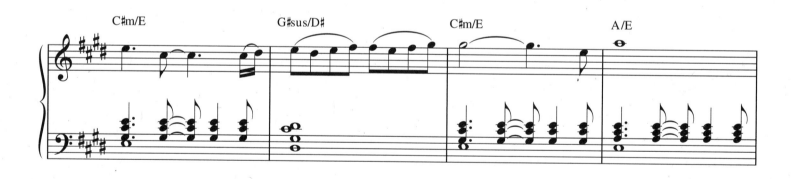

CAN'T FIGHT THE MOONLIGHT

(from *Coyote Ugly*)

Words and Music by
DIANE WARREN

Can't Fight the Moonlight - 5 - 1

Bridge:

Chorus:

COLORBLIND

(from *Invictus*)

Music and Lyrics by
DANIEL PO

Slowly ♩. = 60

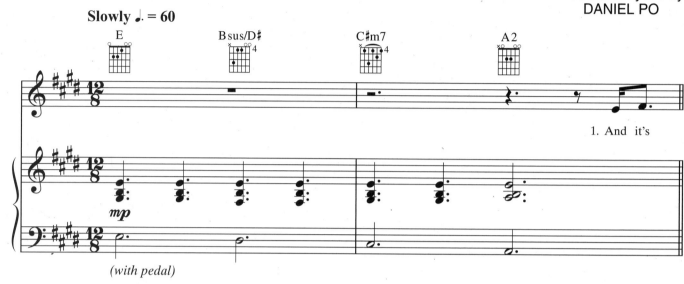

1. And it's

(with pedal)

Verse 1:

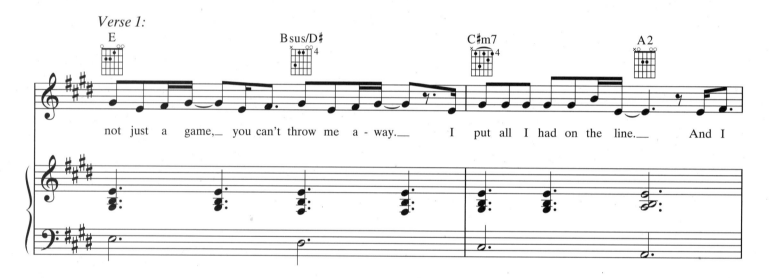

not just a game,__ you can't throw me a-way.__ I put all I had on the line.__ And I

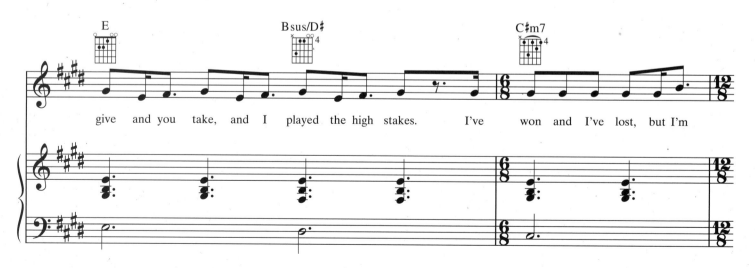

give and you take, and I played the high stakes. I've won and I've lost, but I'm

Colorblind - 6 - 1

COMING HOME FROM THE SEA

(from *The Perfect Storm*)

By JAMES HORNER

Slowly (♩ = 56)

(with pedal)

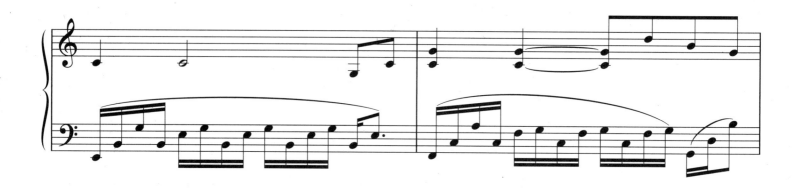

Slightly faster

Broadly (♩ = 108)

Faster (♩ =116)

CONCERNING HOBBITS

(from The Lord of the Rings: The Fellowship of the Ring)

By
HOWARD SHORE

Moderately (♩ = 104)

Warmly (legato)

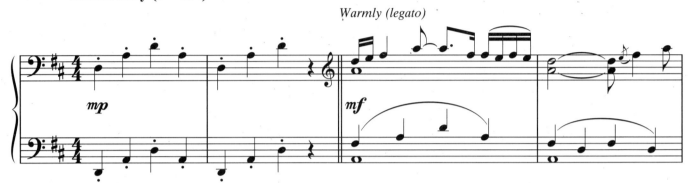

Concerning Hobbits - 4 - 1

CORYNORHINUS
(Surveying the Ruins)
(from *Batman Begins*)

By HANS ZIMMER, JAMES NEWTON HOWARD,
MELVYN WESSON, RAMIN DJAWADI and LORNE BALFE

Moderately slow, rubato (♩ = 72)

(with pedal)

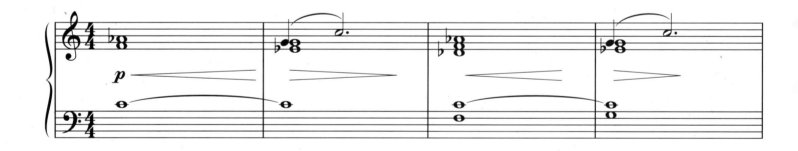

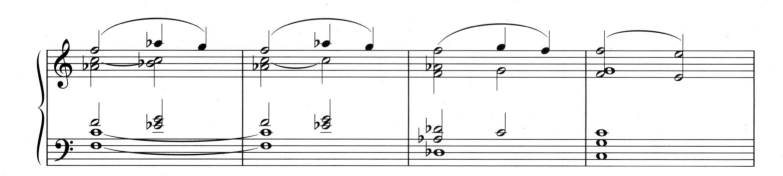

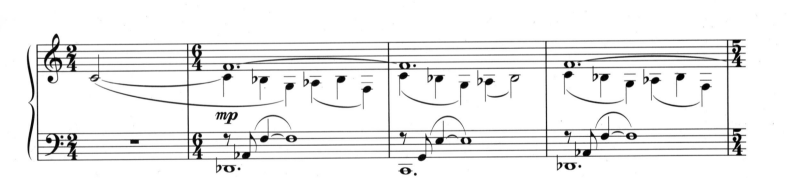

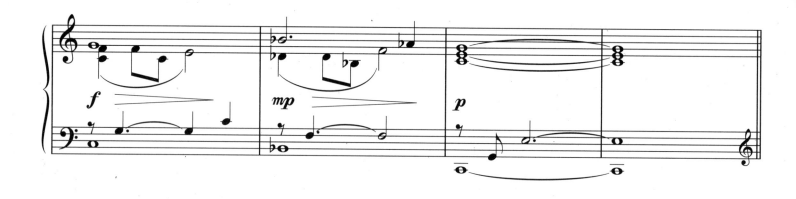

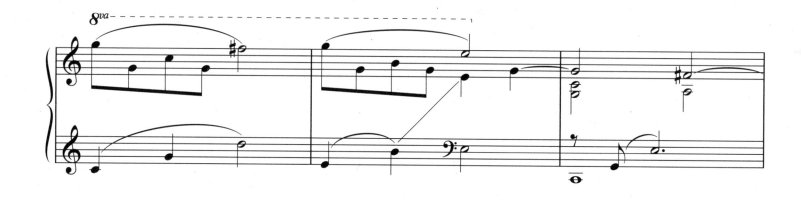

DANCING QUEEN

(from *Mamma Mia!*)

Words and Music by
BENNY ANDERSSON, STIG ANDERSON
and BJÖRN ULVAEUS

Disco rock ♩ = 100

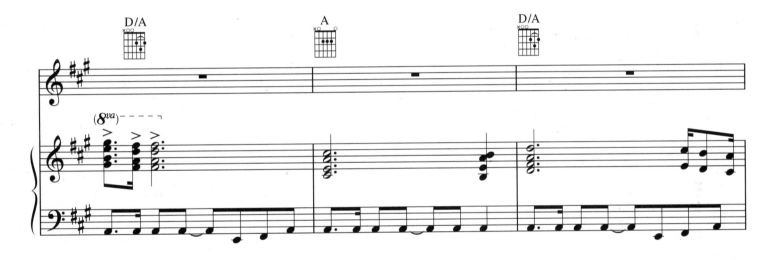

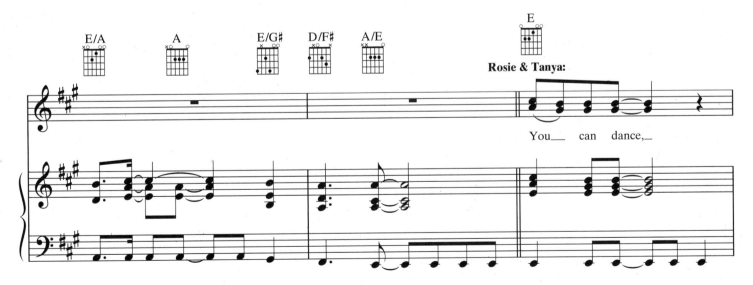

You__ can dance,__

Dancing Queen - 7 - 1

80

DECODE

(from *Twilight*)

Words and Music by
HAYLEY WILLIAMS, JOSH FARRO
and TAYLOR YORK

Moderately slow ♩ = 84

Verse:

1. How can I de-cide___ what's___ right___ when you're cloud-ing up___ my mind?___
2. The truth is hid-ing in___ your___ eyes___ and it's hang-ing on___ your tongue.___

*Original key in B♭m with guitars tuned down a half step.

Decode - 8 - 1

Decode - 8 - 2

My thoughts you can't de - code.)

cresc.

Chorus:

How did we get here

when I used to know__ you__ so__

__ well?__

But how did we get here?

Well, I think I know.__

Bridge:

Do you see___ what we've done?_____ We've gone and made such fools of our - selves._____ Do you see___

mp

what we've done?_____ We've gone and made such

fools of our - selves.

Whoa._____

Chorus:

How did we get here when I used to know__ you__ so_____

DO YOU FEEL ME

(from *American Gangster*)

Words and Music by
DIANE WARREN

Moderately slow ♩ = 84

Verse:

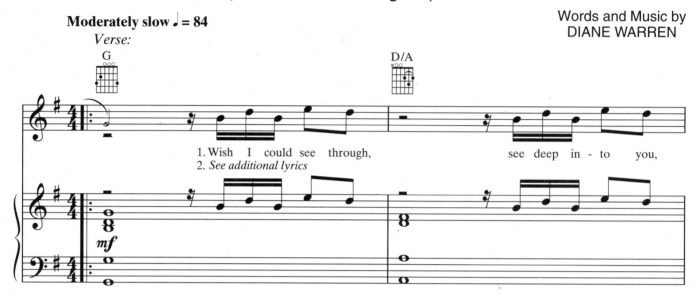

1. Wish I could see through, see deep in - to you,
2. *See additional lyrics*

and know___ what you're think-ing, now._____ And if I'm what you're

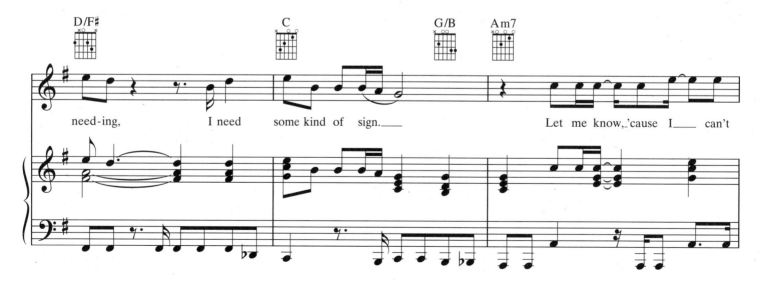

need-ing, I need some kind of sign.___ Let me know, 'cause I___ can't

Do You Feel Me - 6 - 1

Verse 2:
You play it so cool,
Won't let nothing show through,
Won't show what you're feeling.
You like to keep keeping me here in the dark
And I can't see through into your heart.
Let me in, in on the mystery,
'Cause I just can't stay in this guessing game.
(To Chorus:)

THE DARK KNIGHT OVERTURE

(from *The Dark Knight*)

Composed by
HANS ZIMMER and
JAMES NEWTON HOWARD
Arranged by JACK DOLMAN

Mysteriously (♩ = 96)

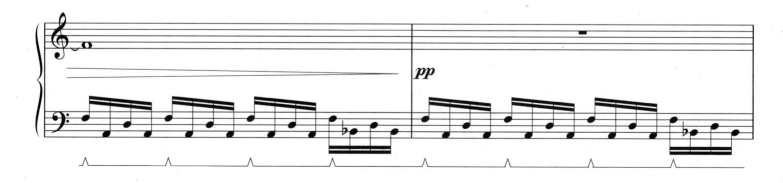

The Dark Knight Overture - 13 - 1

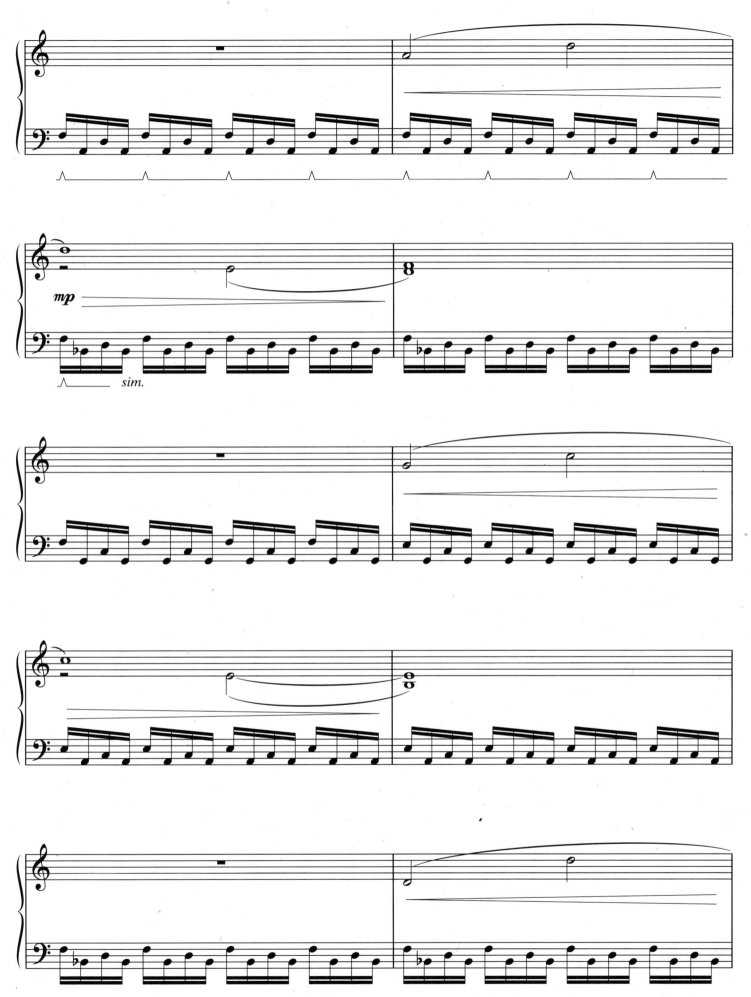

The Dark Knight Overture - 13 - 2

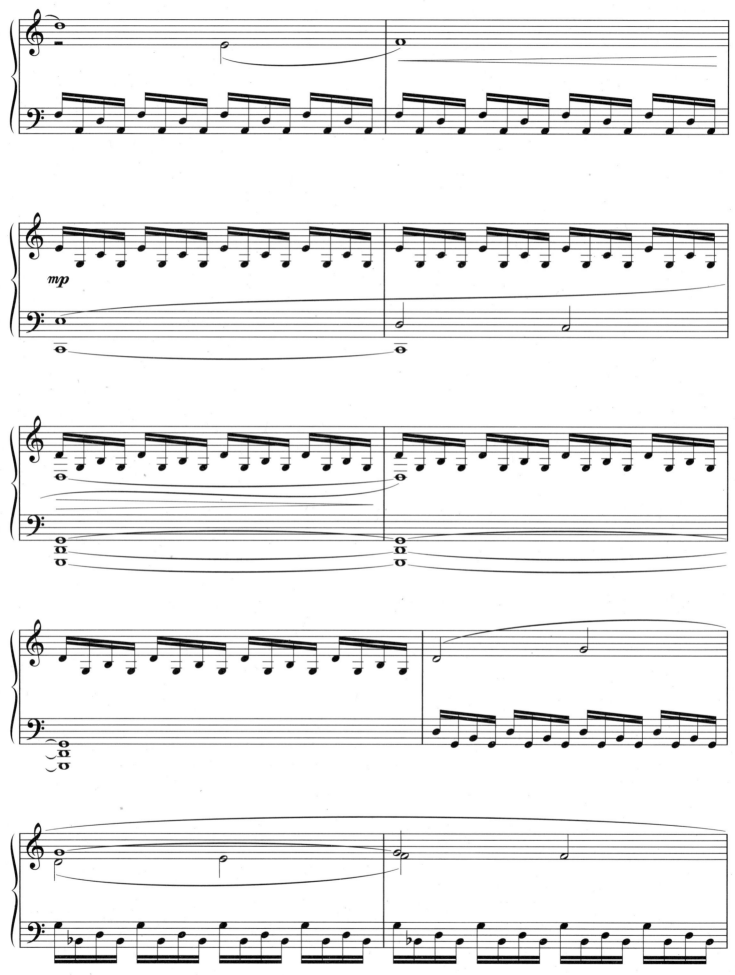

The Dark Knight Overture - 13 - 4

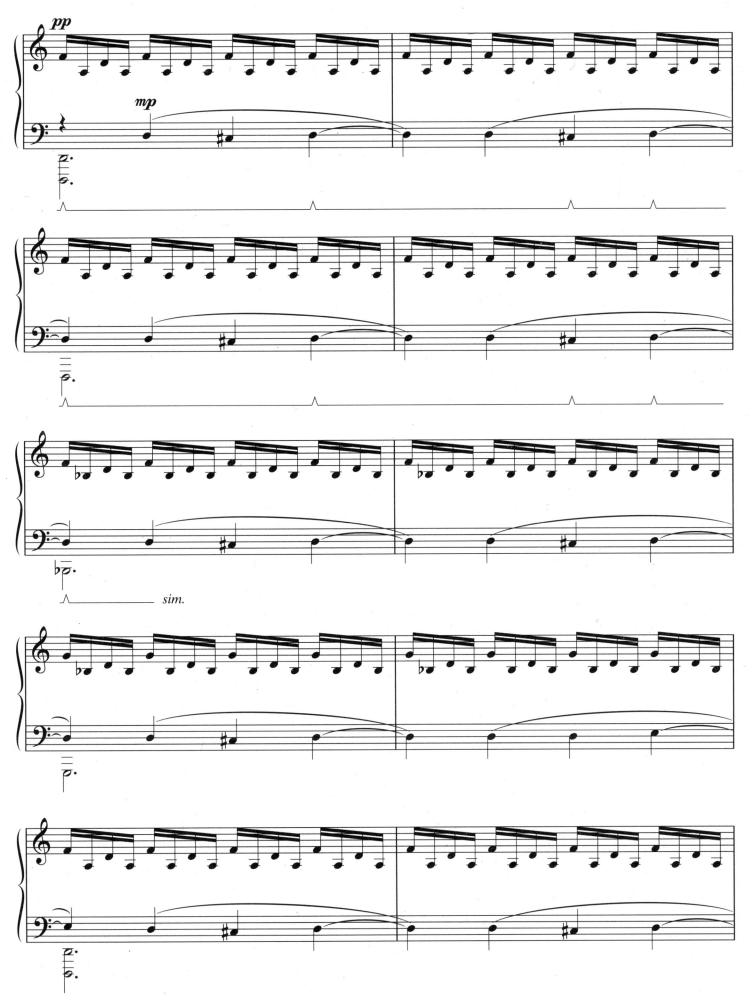

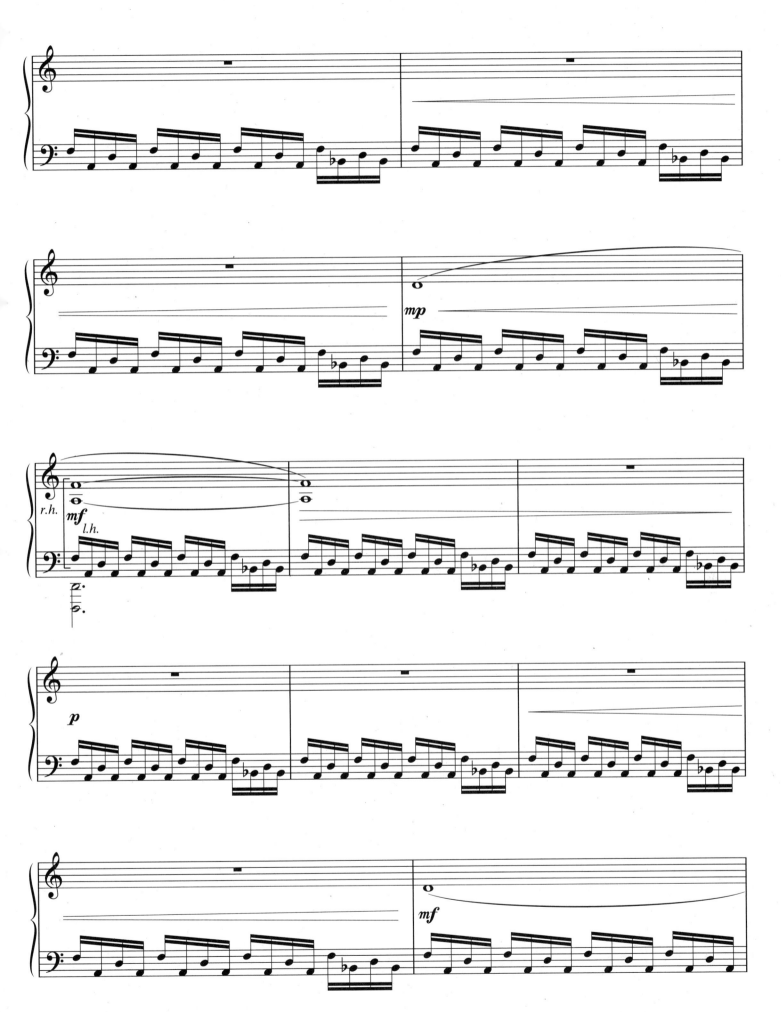

HARRY AND HERMIONE
(from *Harry Potter and the Half-Blood Prince*)

By NICHOLAS HOOPER

Moderately ♩ = 92

FALLING SLOWLY

(from *Once*)

Words and Music by
GLEN HANSARD and
MARKETA IRGLOVA

Slowly ♩ = 69

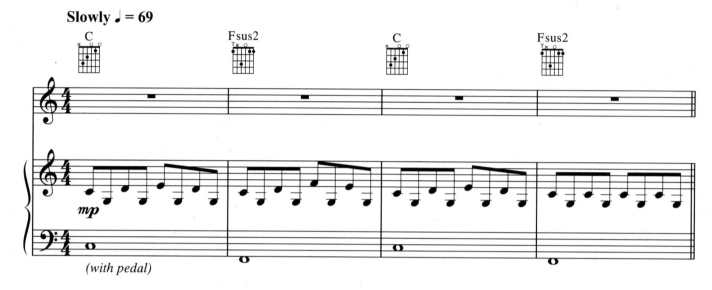

Verse 1:

1. I don't know you, but I want you all the more for that.

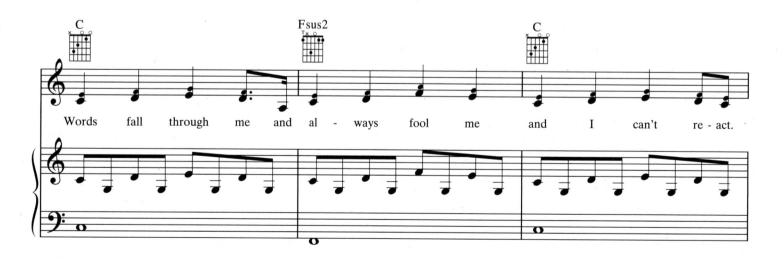

Words fall through me and al - ways fool me and I can't re - act.

Falling Slowly - 6 - 1

FAME

Lyrics by
DEAN PITCHFORD

Music by
MICHAEL GORE

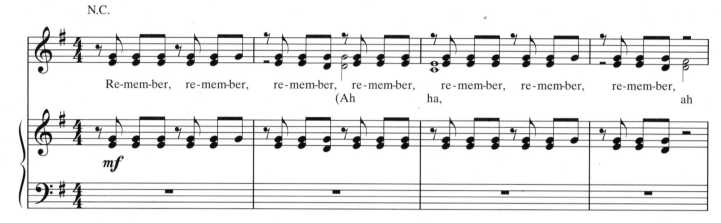

Fame - 6 - 1

FIREWORKS

(from *Harry Potter and the Order of the Phoenix*)

By NICHOLAS HOOPER

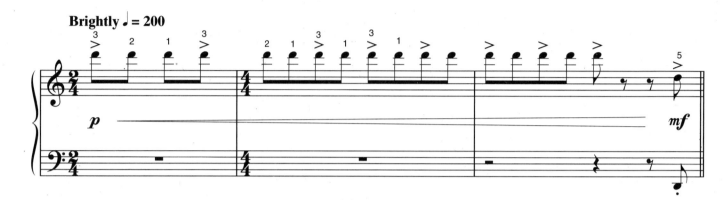

Fireworks - 4 - 1

cresc.

Fireworks - 4 - 4

HARRY'S WONDROUS WORLD

(from *Harry Potter and the Sorcerer's Stone*)

By JOHN WILLIAMS

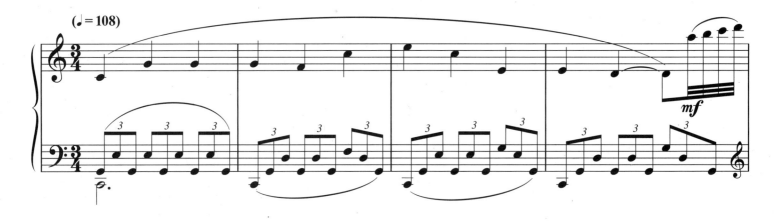

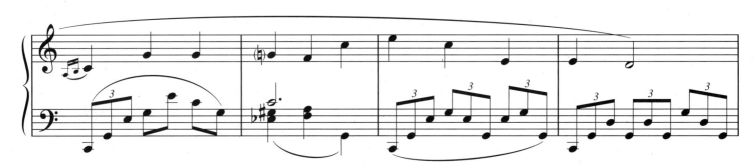

Harry's Wondrous World - 11 - 1

134

Victoriously

HEDWIG'S THEME

(from *Harry Potter and the Sorcerer's Stone*)

By JOHN WILLIAMS

Hedwig's Theme - 5 - 1

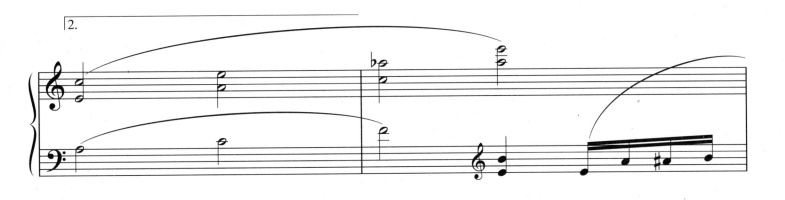

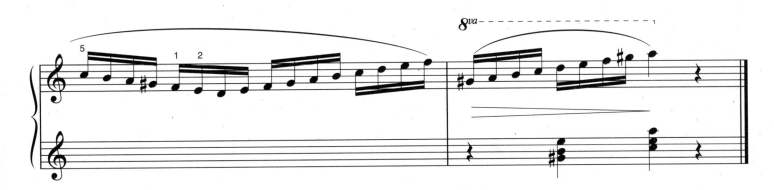

Hedwig's Theme - 5 - 5

HIDEAWAY

(from *Where the Wild Things Are*)

Words and Music by
KAREN O and IMAAD WASIF

Slowly ♩ = 88

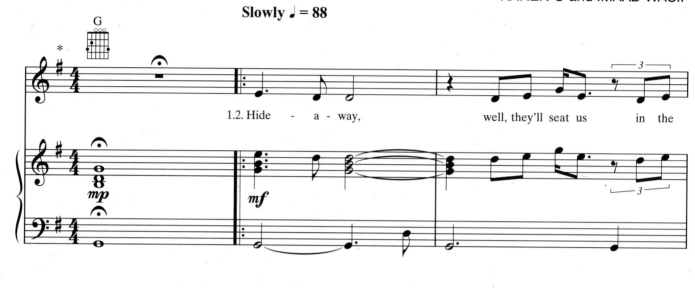

1.2. Hide - a - way, well, they'll seat us in the

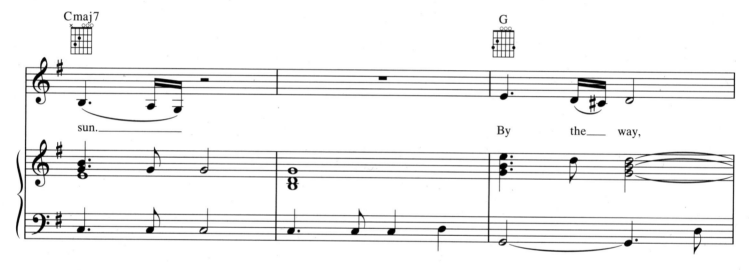

sun. By the way,

know you've al-ways been the one. You'll ask your rea-sons

*Recorded in F♯ major, with guitar tuned down a half step.

Hideaway - 4 - 4

HOGWARTS' HYMN

(from *Harry Potter and the Goblet of Fire*)

By PATRICK DOYLE

Nobilmente con expressivo (♩ = 69)

Hogwarts' Hymn - 3 - 1

Hogwarts' Hymn - 3 - 2

Hogwarts' Hymn - 3 - 3

IF YOU WANT ME

(from *Once*)

Words and Music by
MARKETA IRGLOVA

IN DREAMS
(featured in "The Breaking of the Fellowship")
(from *The Lord of the Rings: The Fellowship of the Ring*)

Words and Music by
FRAN WALSH and
HOWARD SHORE

INTO THE WEST

(from *The Lord of the Rings: The Return of the King*)

Words and Music by
HOWARD SHORE, FRAN WALSH
and ANNIE LENNOX

Moderately ♩ = 92

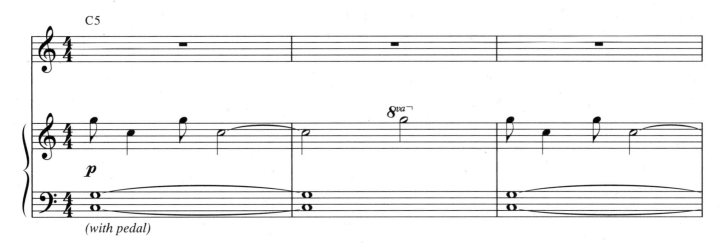

(with pedal)

Verse 1:

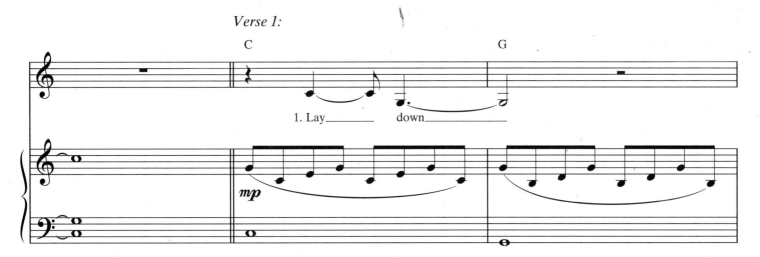

1. Lay_____ down_____

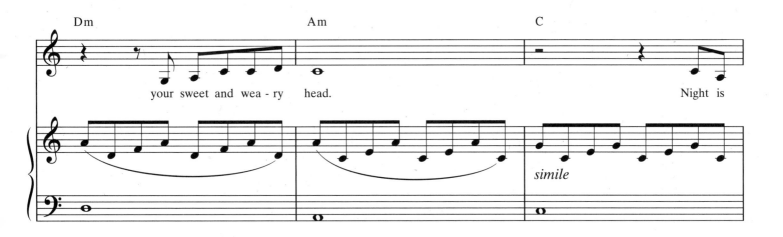

your sweet and wea - ry head.   Night is

simile

Into the West - 9 - 1

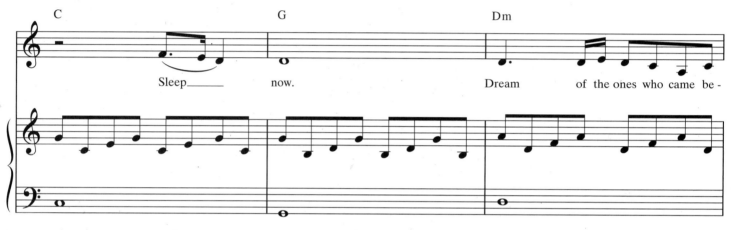

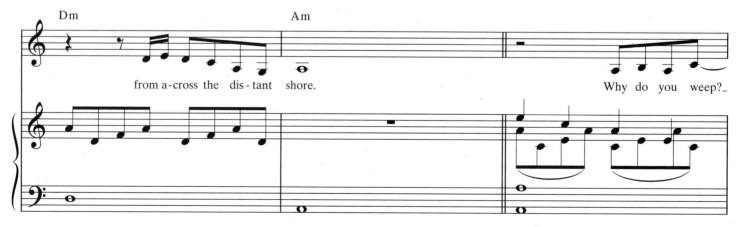

come to car - ry you home.

And all will turn to sil - ver

glass.

A light on the wa - ter,

all souls pass.

Verse 2:

2. Hope___ fades___

mp

Into the West - 9 - 7

IN NOCTEM

(from *Harry Potter and the Half-Blood Prince*)

Lyrics by
STEVE KLOVES

Music by
NICHOLAS HOOPER

Moderately ♪ = 128

Women:

simplice ma espressivo

Car - ry my soul___ in - to the night.___ May the

stars___ light my way.___ I glo - ry

in___ the sight___ as dark - ness takes the

In Noctem - 4 - 1

Men: *lontano (chanting)*

p Fer - te in noc - tem a - ni - mam

me - am I - lust - rent ste - llae vi - am me - am As - pec - tu

i - llo glo - ri - or Dum ca - pit nox di -

LYRA
(from *The Golden Compass*)

Words and Music by
KATE BUSH

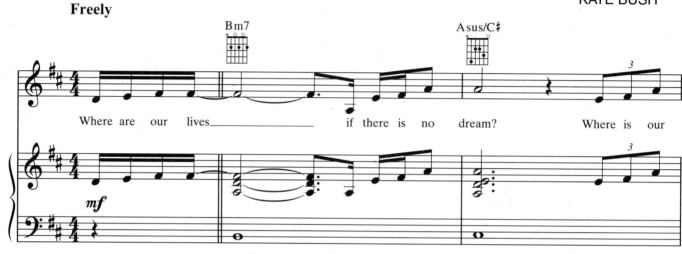

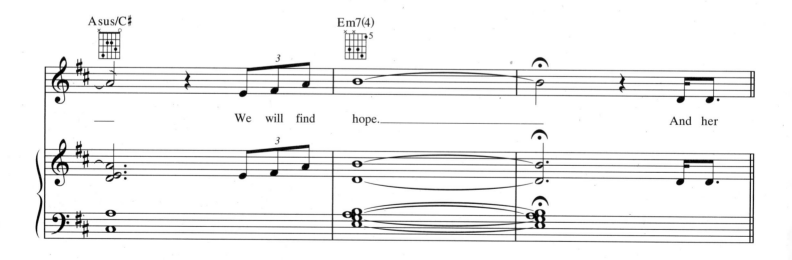

Slowly and freely ♩ = 69

THE HARSHEST PLACE ON EARTH
(Opening Theme from *March of the Penguins*)

By
ALEX WURMAN

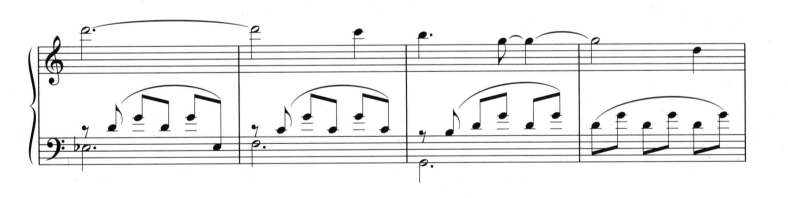

MYSTIC RIVER
(Main Title)

By
CLINT EASTWOOD

Mystic River - 2 - 1

MOVE ON UP

(from *Bend It Like Beckham*)

Words and Music by
CURTIS MAYFIELD

Move On Up - 7 - 1

Verses 2 & 4:

2. Bite your lip___ and take the trip,___ though
4. *See additional lyrics*

there may be___ wet road a - head___ and you can - not slip.___

Just move on up, for peace you'll find.___

Chorus:

Verse 3:
So, hush now, child, and don't you cry.
Your folks might understand you by and by.
Move on up and keep on wishing.
Remember your dream is your only scheme,
So keep on pushing.
(To Interlude:)

Verse 4:
Take nothing less than the supreme best,
Do not obey rumors people say, for you can pass the test.
Just move on up to a greater day.
With just a load of faith, if you put your mind to it,
You can surely do it.
(To Interlude:)

THE NOTEBOOK
(Main Title)

Written by
AARON ZIGMAN

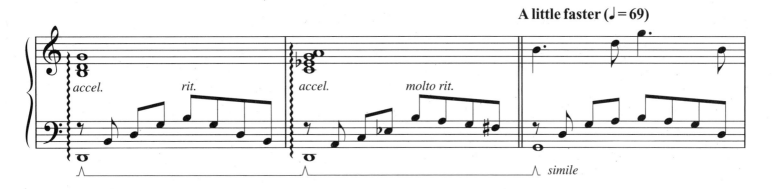

The Notebook - 3 - 1

188

THE PIANO DUET

(from *Corpse Bride*)

Secondo

By DANNY ELFMAN

Slowly, freely (♩. = 44)

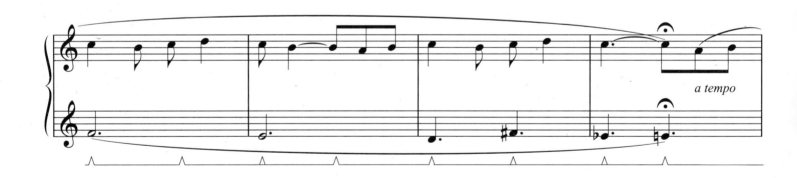

The Piano Duet - 6 - 1

THE PIANO DUET
(from *Corpse Bride*)

Primo

By DANNY ELFMAN

Slowly, freely (♩. = 44)

The Piano Duet - 6 - 2

Secondo

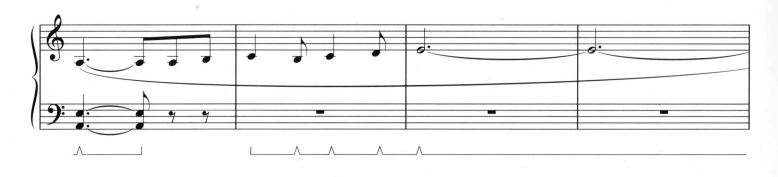

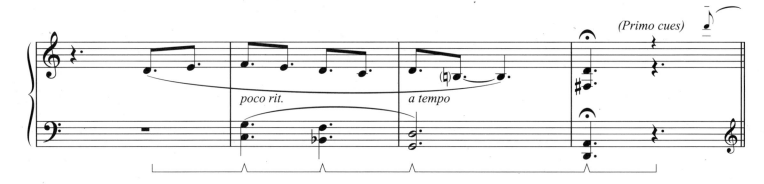

(Primo cues)

poco rit.

a tempo

Brightly (♩. = 92)

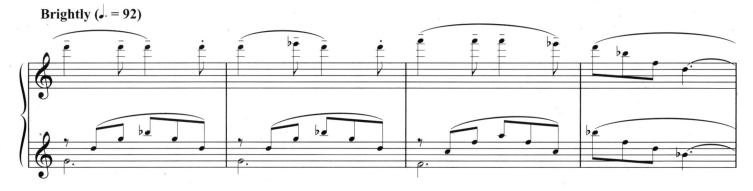

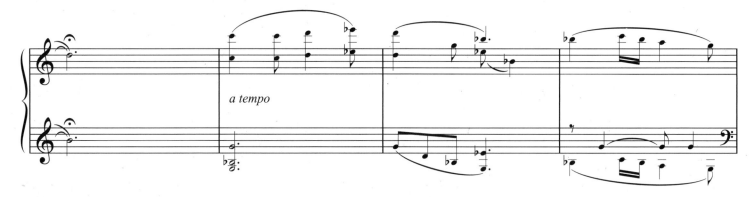

a tempo

Secondo

Slightly slower ($\bullet\! \cdot$ = 80)

Slightly slower ($\bullet\cdot = 80$)

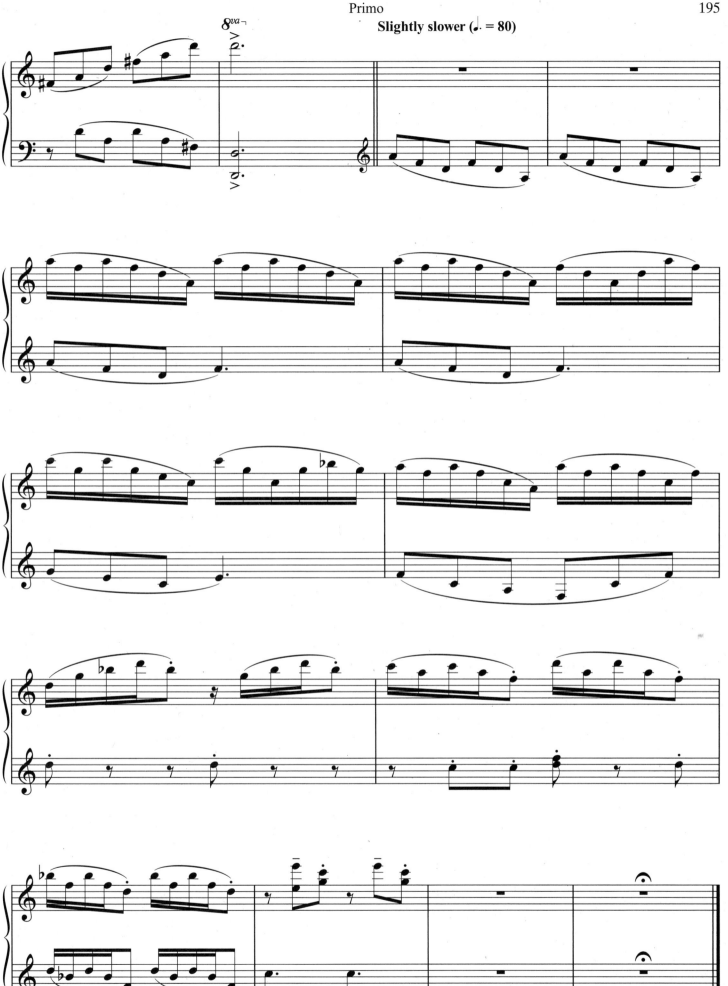

PLATOON SWIMS

(from *Flags of Our Fathers*)

By
CLINT EASTWOOD

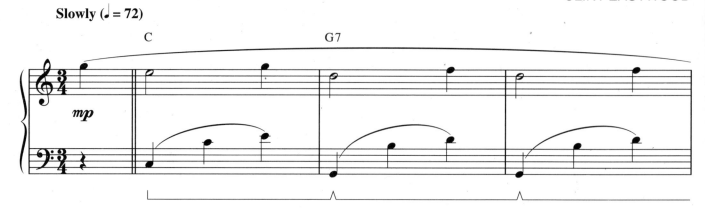

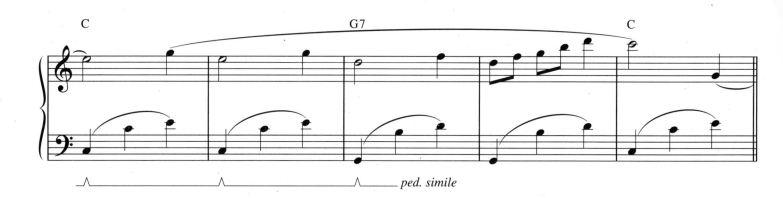

Platoon Swims - 2 - 1

PROM NIGHT

(from *My Sister's Keeper*)

By
AARON ZIGMAN

Slowly and gently (♩ = 80)

THE POSEIDON
(Main Title)

By
KLAUS BADELT

SYRIANA THEME

By ANDRE DESPLAT

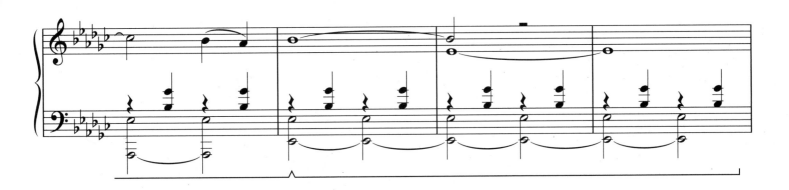

Syriana Theme - 3 - 1

RAIDERS MARCH

(from *Raiders of the Lost Ark*)

Music by
JOHN WILLIAMS

March (♩ = 120)

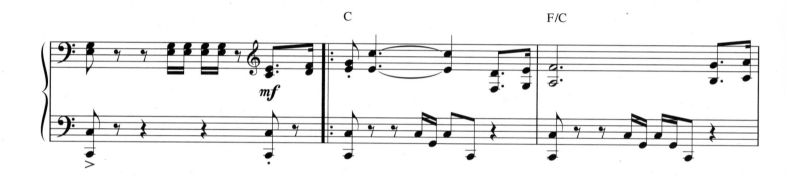

Raiders March - 4 - 1

SEX AND THE CITY
(Main Title Theme)

By DOUGLAS CUOMO

Bright latin ♩ = 157

Sex and the City - 2 - 1

STAR WARS
(Main Title)

By JOHN WILLIAMS

Majestically, steady march (♩ = 108)

Star Wars - 4 - 1

THEME FROM "SUPERMAN"

By JOHN WILLIAMS

Theme From "Superman" - 4 - 1

Theme From "Superman" - 4 - 4

THANK YOU FOR THE MUSIC

(from *Mamma Mia!*)

Words and Music by
BENNY ANDERSSON,
STIG ANDERSON and BJÖRN ULVAEUS

THIS IS IT

(from *Michael Jackson's This Is It*)

Written and Composed by
MICHAEL JACKSON
and PAUL ANKA

Moderately ♩ = 96

(with pedal)

Verse:

1. This is it;_____ here I stand._____ I'm the light_
(2.) I can say_____ I'm the light_
(3.) I can feel_____ I'm the light_

____ of the world;____ I feel grand._____ Got this love____
____ of the world;____ run a - way._____ We can feel____
____ of the world;____ this is real._____ Feel my song;____

This Is It - 4 - 1

VICTOR'S PIANO SOLO

(from *Corpse Bride*)

By DANNY ELFMAN

Victor's Piano Solo - 2 - 1

*F𝄪 = G♮

THERE YOU'LL BE

(from *Pearl Harbor*)

Words and Music by
DIANE WARREN

There You'll Be - 5 - 1

Ab   Eb/G   Fm   Eb

___ I'll keep___ a part___ of you___ with me.___ And ev -

1.

Db   Ab/C   Bbm7   Absus   Ab

'ry - where___ I am,___ there you'll be.___ And ev -

Db   Ab/C   Bbm7   Ab   Gb(9)   Db(9)/F

'ry - where_ I am,___ there you'll be.___ 2. Well, you

2.   Bridge:

Db   Ab/C   Bbm7   Eb   Ab

'ry - where___ I am,___ there you'll be.___ 'Cuz I al - ways saw in you___ my light,___

WAY BACK INTO LOVE

(from *Music and Lyrics*)

Words and Music by
ADAM SCHLESINGER

Moderately ♩ = 104

Verses 1 & 2:

Female: 1. I've been liv-ing with a shad-ow o-ver head. I've been sleep-ing with a
Male: 2. I've been hid-ing all my hopes and dreams a-way, just in case I ev-er

cloud a-bove my bed. I've been lone-ly for so long,
need 'em a-gain some day. I've been set-ting a-side time to

Way Back Into Love - 7 - 5

WONKA'S WELCOME SONG

(from *Charlie and the Chocolate Factory*)

Lyrics by
JOHN AUGUST and
DANNY ELFMAN

Music by
DANNY ELFMAN

Wonka's Welcome Song - 4 - 1

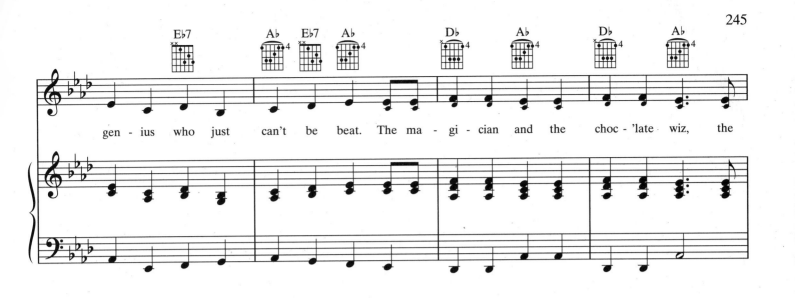

gen - ius who just can't be beat. The ma - gi - cian and the choc - 'late wiz, the

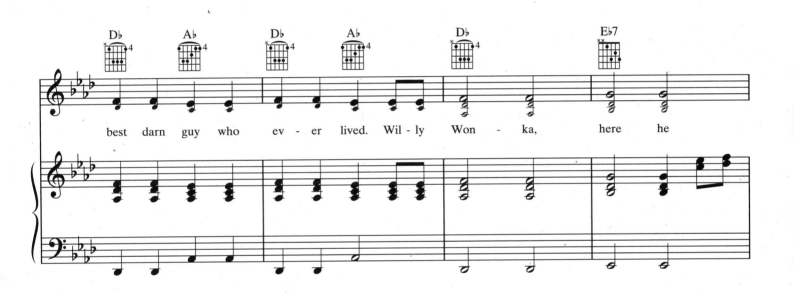

best darn guy who ev - er lived. Wil - ly Won - ka, here he

is! _____

THE WRESTLER

Words and Music by
BRUCE SPRINGSTEEN

250

bruis - es I dis - play.

3. Have you

Verse 3:

ev - er seen a one - leg - ged man try'n' to dance__ his way free?__ If you've

ev - er seen a one - leg - ged man, then you've__ seen me.

Repeat ad lib. and fade

The Wrestler - 6 - 6

WHEN YOUR MIND'S MADE UP

(from *Once*)

Words and Music by
GLEN HANSARD